AMBROISE METHOD 1.0

AMBROISE METHOD 1.0

A Short Easy-to-Use Guide on Revolutionary Debt Repayment

JAMES AMBROISE

gatekeeper press™
Tampa, Florida

The views and opinions expressed in this book are solely those of the author and do not necessarily reflect the views or opinions of Gatekeeper Press. Gatekeeper Press is not to be held responsible for and expressly disclaims responsibility for the content herein.

Ambroise Method 1-0: A Short Easy-to-Use Guide on Revolutionary Debt Repayment

Published by Gatekeeper Press
7853 Gunn Hwy., Suite 209
Tampa, FL 33626
www.GatekeeperPress.com

Copyright © 2023 by James Ambroise
All rights reserved. Neither this book, nor any parts within it may be sold or reproduced in any form or by any electronic or mechanical means, including information storage and retrieval systems, without permission in writing from the author. The only exception is by a reviewer, who may quote short excerpts in a review.

Library of Congress Control Number: 2023940345

ISBN paperback: 9781662941238
eISBN: 9781662941245

America, good morning. My name is James Ambroise. By the grace of God, I devised the greatest debt repayment method ever known to man, at least at the natural level, and the name of the debt repayment method is:

Ambroise Method 1.0

This method when implemented properly will produce exceptional, phenomenal results regarding interest savings or saving the most interest costs, which may allow us to get ahead of the three popular debt repayment methods out there: Debt Snowball, Debt Avalanche, Velocity Banking.

My method will or may cure the imperfection of Debt Snowball in terms of reducing interest costs.

My method will or may cure the imperfection of Debt Avalanche in terms of reducing interest costs.

My method will or may cure the imperfection of Velocity Banking in terms of reducing interest costs.

I have created different examples or case studies to prove my claim, and before we get to the examples or case studies, please allow me to offer my new Anthem Prayer:

Jesus, my Lord, my God, my Creator
I now know that it's not by might, nor by power
so give me the grace to overcome all temptations
give me the grace not to yield to any temptations
give me the grace, Oh Lord, to follow your precepts

My spirit is willing, but my flesh is weak
so take more of me, give me more of you, Lord
More of your faithfulness
More of your hope
More of your love, in Jesus's name
Amen!

Here are some of my credentials, to satisfy the readers who may care about this. I have been or am a bookkeeper and accountant, QuickBooks Pro advisor online, senior tax advisor, real estate investor (single-family residence), residential property manager (for my own residential property portfolio), and a financial coach.

My method, Ambroise Method 1.0, was born out of the necessities of knowing that 84% of U.S. adults had or have a credit card; however, 64% of Americans are living paycheck to paycheck. Even worse, based on statistics released by the Federal Reserve, when Americans are faced with a hypothetical expense of $400, about 68% of all adults in 2021 said that they would have covered it exclusively with cash, savings, or a credit card paid off at the next statement. The remainder said they would have paid by borrowing or selling something or said they would not have been able to cover the expense at all.

Truly, as you can see, small, unexpected expenses can be a hardship for many families. Most Americans do not have cash flow or enough money leftover to cover these small expenses, like a car repair or a modest medical bill.

Most of the traditional debt pay down methods or debt repayment methods focus solely on cash flow or money leftover to pay down a debt or multiple, small debts, or coming up with a large payment to attack debt(s). Based on the statistics presented earlier, the vast majority of Americans clearly do not have enough cash flow or money leftover to fully execute some of these methods, let alone have the ability to send in a large payment to pay down/off debt(s).

Assuming for a second that they do have the funds to pay down/off debt(s), we will attempt to pick apart the imperfections of each of the three popular methods out there, and how we may easily beat their numbers or get ahead in terms of reducing interest costs.

Debt Snowball in part calls for paying down/off debt from smallest balance to largest balance, and the cash flow gains from the smallest balance debt will then be rolled over into the next debt repayment. Let me preface this by saying that the debt snowball group had the foresight to know that their method may not yield the best outcome in terms of reducing interest costs; interest savings is not their main focus or aim. Even though our method and debt snowball share two distinct philosophies, we believe that their method complements ours in the sense that they are telling Americans not to borrow or borrow less, not to even get into credit card debt, which probably covers a small percentage of us. Here we're trying to cover the remaining percentage; we are telling them that in the case that they did not follow that plan, they've already borrowed a lot or had too many credit cards and personal loans. Here's a way to get out of debt faster and garner the most interest savings based on current interest computation rules in the year 2023 compared to any other methods out there. In a way, this group is attacking the big banks, the big creditors one way, and here we will attack the big banks, the big creditors' bottom line a separate way; after all, we have a bigger percentage of the population that do borrow or have lot of credit cards and personal loan debts. Indeed, their method and ours complement each other in that sense.

We will go easy on debt snowball since interest saving is not their aim. The example below is one of the ways we could amicably surpass their results in terms of reducing interest costs:

List of Debts	Credit Limit	APR	Bal Owed	Min.	Avail	Credit Utilization	Payment Rate Charged
Wells Fargo Platinum Credit Card	5,000	20.00%	4,000	80	1,000	80.00%	2.00%
Capital One Credit Card	7,230	24.00%	6,000	120	1,230	82.99%	2.00%
Chase Sapphire Pref Credit Card	11,364	21.00%	10,000	200	1,364	88.00%	2.00%
NavyFederal Credit Card	21,000	15.00%	18,540	371	2,460	88.29%	2.00%

Extra payment/Money leftover: $3

Assuming that the folks who subscribe to the debt snowball method have $10,000 available to pay down/off debts in the form of an income tax refund, a cash gift from loved ones, etc.

With that $10,000, they may then pay Wells Fargo Platinum's $4000 and Capital One's $6000 balance.

Let us see how much interest they were able to save by getting rid of those two debts if they were carrying this hypothetical balance for an entire year.

To keep math simple, we will compare over the course of one year.

Four thousand dollars at 20% interest or $4,000 x 20/100 is $800 of interest savings—gaining the $80 minimum payment in the process.

Six thousand dollars at 24% interest or $6,000 x 24/100 is $1,440 of interest savings—gaining $120 minimum payment in the process.

In total, they would save $800 + $1,440 or $2,240 in interest for the year—they will be gaining $200 total minimum payment(s) in the process.

To get everybody up to speed, let us joyfully acquaint you with a new term: Ambroise's partitioning a balance.

Ambroise's partitioning a balance is to divide the balance into at least two separate parts, where one of the parts will equal the other account or credit card balance we are trying to compare it with.

Now, let us partition the balance of Chase Sapphire credit card $10,000 at 21% or $2,100 yearly interest, which is the same as:

Six thousand dollars at 21% or $1,260 in yearly interest charges from Chase Sapphire credit card.

+

Four thousand dollars at 21% or $840 in yearly interest charges from Chase Sapphire credit card. (This portion from Chase's $4,000 balance is being compared with Wells Fargo's $4,000 balance.)

When you have added the two, $1260 and $840 in yearly interest charges from Chase Sapphire credit card, our proof result is the same for the original Chase Sapphire—$2,100 yearly interests.

Armed with that information, we will instead pay down/off these debts below with the same $10,000.

Capital One—$6000 at 24% interest or $6,000 x 24/100 is $1,440 of interest savings. Gaining $120 minimum payment in the process.

Chase Sapphire for a partial payment of $4,000 at 21% or $4,000 x 21/100 is $840—gaining $80 minimum payment in the process since this payment will reduce the minimum due from $200 to $120.

In total, we would save $1,440 + $840 or $2,280 in interest charges for the year. We will also be gaining $200 total minimum payment(s) in the process.

We were able to save $2,280 in interest, gaining $200 minimum payment in the process while the debt snowball group was able to only save $2,240 in interests, also gaining $200 minimum payment in the process. In this example, we have achieved $40 more in interest savings compared to debt snowball.

Note: When comparing two separate revolving credit accounts, the so-called snowball effect is achieved whether one account is paid off in full and the other account is paid off partially; thus, cash flow is increased in both scenarios.

The original Excel worksheet looked like this before any adjustment:

List of Debts	Credit Limit	APR	Bal Owed	Min.	Avail	Credit Utilization	Payment Rate Charged
Wells Fargo Platinum Credit Card	5,000	20.00%	4,000	80	1,000	80.00%	2.00%
Capital One Credit Card	7,230	24.00%	6,000	120	1,230	82.99%	2.00%
Chase Sapphire Pref Credit Card	11,364	21.00%	10,000	200	1,364	88.00%	2.00%
NavyFederal Credit Card	21,000	15.00%	18,540	371	2,460	88.29%	2.00%

Debt snowball did not come on top in terms of interest savings.

Debt snowball—adjusted Excel worksheet will look something like this:

List of Debts	Credit Limit	APR	Bal Owed	Min.	Avail	Credit Utilization	Payment Rate Charged
Wells Fargo Platinum Credit Card	5,000	20.00%	0	0	5,000	0.00%	0.00%
Capital One Credit Card	7,230	24.00%	0	0	7,230	0.00%	0.00%
Chase Sapphire Pref Credit Card	11,364	21.00%	10,000	200	1,364	88.00%	2.00%
NavyFederal Credit Card	21,000	15.00%	18,540	371	2,460	88.29%	2.00%

Our own adjusted Excel worksheet will look something like this:

List of Debts	Credit Limit	APR	Bal Owed	Min.	Avail	Credit Utilization	Payment Rate Charged
Wells Fargo Platinum Credit Card	5,000	20.00%	4,000	80	1,000	80.00%	2.00%
Capital One Credit Card	7,230	24.00%	0	0	7,230	0.00%	0.00%
Chase Sapphire Pref Credit Card	11,364	21.00%	6,000	120	5,364	52.80%	2.00%
NavyFederal Credit Card	21,000	15.00%	18,540	371	2,460	88.29%	2.00%

Again, this is only one of the many ways we may surpass the results from this debt snowball group in terms of reducing overall interest costs.

As you can see, we did not inflate the numbers from the original example or case study in order to make our results look more impressive.

Our Observations:

Debt snowball method uses only cash flow or extra payment; this group is not concerned with higher interest rate debts. Debt snowball does not go far enough in eliminating debts quickly, since this group does not take advantage of different types of balance transfers between current, existing accounts, if any, and does not utilize alternative account(s). These strategies and techniques will be fully explained later in the book.

Let us now move on to another popular debt method: the debt avalanche.

Debt Avalanche in part calls for paying down/off debt from highest interest rate or APR first. In other words, you will use any available funds to pay the debt with the highest interest rate.

The example below is one of the ways we can do better than debt avalanche in terms of reducing interest costs:

List of Debts	APR	Bal Owed	Payment	Payment Rate Charged	Current Terms In months
Best Egg Personal Loan	23.00%	10000	387	3.87%	1 of 36 months
Wells Fargo Credit Card	21.00%	10000	387	3.87%	
Capital One Credit Card	15.68%	10000	387	3.87%	
Chase Credit Card	15.00%	10000	387	3.87%	

Cashflow: $3

If the folks who subscribe to debt avalanche method have $10,000 in funds available to pay down/off debts in the form of an income tax refund, a cash gift from loved ones, etc.

With that $10,000, they will surely pay off Best Egg personal loan; after all, Best Egg's 23% rate is by far the highest APR compared to the rest of the debts on the list.

Let us see how much interest they would be able to save by getting rid of Best Egg personal loan if they were carrying this hypothetical balance for an entire year.

Again, to keep math simple, we will compute this over the course of one year. As you may already know, installment credit and revolving credit interests are computed differently. Best Egg personal loan in this case is an installment credit or loan, which means that of the $387 monthly payment, part of this payment will go to principal and the other part will go to interest.

Best Egg Personal Loan	Beginning Balance	Interest	Principal	Ending Balance
1	$10,000.00	$191.67	$195.43	$9,804.57
2	$9,804.57	$187.92	$199.18	$9,605.39
3	$9,605.39	$184.10	$203.00	$9,402.40
4	$9,402.40	$180.21	$206.89	$9,195.51
5	$9,195.51	$176.25	$210.85	$8,984.66
6	$8,984.66	$172.21	$214.89	$8,769.77
7	$8,769.77	$168.09	$219.01	$8,550.76
8	$8,550.76	$163.89	$223.21	$8,327.56
9	$8,327.56	$159.61	$227.49	$8,100.07
10	$8,100.07	$155.25	$231.85	$7,868.22
11	$7,868.22	$150.81	$236.29	$7,631.94
12	$7,631.94	$146.28	$240.82	$7,391.10

This is the breakdown for interest charges from Best Egg in year one, and the total interest charges from Best Egg over a 12-month period would be about $2,036.

The debt avalanche group, for paying off the highest interest rate first, would get $2,036 in interest savings over 12 months.

It is noted that you may have to compare two separate accounts for a much shorter period than 12 months. In every scenario, you have to first run the numbers to determine the highest interest savings, and based on your findings, you can then proceed in sending extra payments to the right account.

Our process here is slightly different than the debt avalanche. We will go for interest rate (APR) when it makes more (number, math) sense to do so; otherwise we will certainly go for interest charges instead.

Wells Fargo credit card—$10,000 at 21% or $10,000 x 21/100 is $2,100 in yearly interest. Debt avalanche—going after the highest APR Best Egg would save $2,036 in interest.

With our process of going after the highest interest charges, Wells Fargo credit card would do better with $2,100 in interest savings.

This is one of the many ways we will get greater results than the debt avalanche. Again, we did not inflate the numbers from the original example in order to make our results look more impressive.

Our Observations:

Like debt snowball, the debt avalanche method uses cash flow or extra payment only. Debt avalanche does not go far enough in eliminating debts quickly since this group does not take advantage of different types of balance transfers between current, existing accounts, if any, and does not utilize alternative account(s). Again, these strategies and techniques will be fully explained later in the book.

So far, we were able to do better than both the debt snowball and debt avalanche methods. There is still one more debt repayment method floating out there—velocity banking.

In this next section, we will tackle in greater detail a more complex issue: the so-called debt weapon. America, if you prefer to utilize a regular checking or savings account to pay down/off debts instead of employing an alternative deposit or alternative withdrawal account, this next section may not apply to you.

In all honesty, velocity banking itself is a good concept. However, we will attempt to go over some of the possible deficiencies or pitfalls that may be associated with this plan or method. More specifically, which alternative account we should use in a case where we have more than one to choose from and/or which account gets to keep the cash flow/extra payment at the end.

Velocity Banking—this group in part looks to acquire a new or use an existing so-called debt weapon, preferably one that offers greater liquidity. In the case of a home equity line of credit (HELOC), personal line of credit, or credit card as a debt weapon, they may use that account whenever possible to chunk or send a large payment toward other debts. Any new, total available cash flow will be used to zero out the debt weapon or close to zero out the debt weapon, so they could start the process of chunking or sending large payments again toward remaining debts. The movements of income coming into the account and expenses going out from that (alternative) account will no doubt reduce the overall interest rate from that account.

Here is an example using one of this group's preferred debt weapons, the HELOC:

List of Debts	Limit	APR	Bal Owed	Min.	Avail	Credit Utilization	Payment Rate Charged	Term In Years
Wells Fargo Platinum	5,000	20.00%	4,000	80	1,000	80.00%	2.00%	
Capital One credit card	7,230	24.00%	6,000	120	1,230	82.99%	2.00%	
Chase Sapphire Pref	11,364	21.00%	10,000	200	1,364	88.00%	2.00%	
NavyFederal Loan	21,000	2.50%	21,000	460	0	100.00%	2.19%	4
Regions HELOC	50,000	3.99%	30,000	99.75	20,000	60.00%	0.33%	1 of 10
Interfirst Mortgage	116,350	3.99%	116,000	806	350	99.70%	0.69%	30

Income: $2,500 Expense: $2,300 Debts: $187,000

Cash flow/Money leftover: $200

The velocity banking group may pick the wrong so-called debt weapon, especially in the case where there are multiple debt weapons to choose from. This group at times may fixate or pay too much attention to the account that they could chunk out of, Regions HELOC in this example; after all, Regions HELOC has the biggest availability of funds available to use.

Their debt weapon more than likely may be Regions HELOC.

Ambroise method 1.0 follows an unrelated process and offers a greater outcome for reducing interest costs while getting out of debt exceptionally faster than any other method out there. Using a regular checking or savings account to strategically pay down/off debts is all you will need, America.

However, if an alternative account must be employed, our terminology and processes are vastly different. Even though it is not required, we almost always use an alternative deposit or alternative withdrawal account (ADAWA), an account that works similarly to a checking account, and we have a wholistic approach on how we look at debts and how we pay down/off debts. Our debt repayment method truly is second to none.

We attempt to offer greater, faster relief for the 64% of Americans who are living paycheck to paycheck; the 68% of us who may not be able to cover a $400 emergency, based on the Federal Reserve statistics.

Keep these in mind!

	Chase Credit Card, in this example	**Regions HELOC, in this example**
Type	Revolving	Revolving in this case (draw period remaining)
Computation	Average daily	Average daily
Liquidity	May or may not be as liquid	Greater liquidity (draw period remaining)
Term Left	N/A	We are in year 1 of 10-year draw

Let us introduce some new terminologies:

FIRST IN LINE alternative account—for our purpose, it is the account that offers greater results in reducing interest costs compared to another alternative account on a given list.

NEXT IN LINE alternative account—for our purpose, it is the account that offers greater liquidity compared to another alternative account on a given list.

Note: There are times where one account offers both greater liquidity and greater results in reducing interest costs.

Comparing the Other Debt Repayment Methods Against Themselves

Looking carefully online at the application of velocity banking, this group often gets superior results and does extremely well against the other two methods, debt snowball and debt avalanche, and other times this group loses or barely breaks even when compared with debt snowball and/or debt avalanche.

Based on these observations, we wanted to dive deeply into the reason why the use of a debt weapon in part performed great in some instances but performed poorly in other instances.

By the grace of God, we believe that we have partially come across a breakthrough:

The movements of income coming into that (alternative) account and expenses going out of that (alternative) account is partly where the problem lies and depends on the scenario the debt weapon may only be valuable up to a certain point. In other words, the timing of income going into that account and expenses leaving that account should be carefully examined, and the amount of cash flow, if any at all, may be better served somewhere else. Simply put, cash flow may have to go to a different account or debt. We will explain further below, and we will break down these two potential issues one by one.

The Movements of Income and Expenses from That Alternative Account

A survey revealed that the biweekly pay period is the most common, followed by weekly, then semimonthly, then monthly. Certain pay periods tend to dominate in individual industries, an example being the use of weekly pay periods by 82.4 percent of construction establishments.

(Source: U.S. Bureau of Labor Statistics, Current Employment Statistics survey.)

Since biweekly pay period is the most common, we will concentrate on that for now.

While an individual is waiting to receive the next biweekly paycheck or income, the bills have not stopped; they keep coming or are due throughout the month, and this may create problems in this alternative account when expenses going out surpass income coming in, even for a brief period. Too many expenses going out of the alternative account may increase the overall balance, which in turn will diminish the performance of that account. Remember that interest on a PLOC, HELOC, or credit card, to name a few, is calculated mostly (average) daily.

That can prove to get worse for people who are on commissions, salaries, or irregular-type paychecks. To alleviate this problem to some extent, one option is to change the respective due dates of those bills.

However, this may not solve anything. It depends on the type of pay period you are in and small financial emergencies that always seem to arise. Another option is to charge your credit card for bills that can go on a credit card, then pay at least the statement balance for the given credit card on or before the due date. Here a possible residual interest or trailing interest may create problems.

Cash Flow or Extra Payment

As mentioned earlier, depending on the scenario the debt weapon may only be valuable up to a certain point. Cash flow/extra payment may be better served somewhere else. Simply put, cash flow should go to a different account or debt.

We are in effect saying that, yes, if the debt weapon or our ADAWA account offers greater liquidity only, it should receive some of the income initially to reduce the overall rate of this NEXT IN LINE alternative account even further. However, this depends on the scenario; the debt weapon or our ADAWA account may or may not keep the cash flow or extra payment at the end.

Finally, we will demonstrate, using an Excel worksheet, a brief, quick application of an alternative deposit, alternative withdrawal account, and which account or debt truly deserves to keep at a minimum the cash flow or extra payment.

Let us now run the numbers:

List of Debts	Limit	APR	Bal Owed	Min.	Avail	Credit Utilization	Payment Rate Charged	Term In Years
Wells Fargo Platinum	5,000	20.00%	4,000	80	1,000	80.00%	2.00%	
Capital One Credit Card	7,230	24.00%	6,000	120	1,230	82.99%	2.00%	
Chase Sapphire Pref	11,364	21.00%	10,000	200	1,364	88.00%	2.00%	
NavyFederal Loan	21,000	2.50%	21,000	460	0	100.00%	2.19%	4
Regions HELOC	50,000	3.99%	30,000	99.75	20,000	60.00%	0.33%	1 of 10
Interfirst Mortgage	116,350	3.99%	116,000	806	350	99.70%	0.69%	30

Income: $2,500 Expense: $2,300 Debts: $187,000

Cash flow/Money leftover: $200

Using Regions HELOC as a debt weapon, this group may start right away with a chunk or chunking; after all, the formula for cash flow is too small, not comparable.

Now, assuming that they are willing to take advantage of 80% of Regions HELOC limit,

$50,000 x 80% minus current balance of $30,000, so $10,000 is available for a large payment or chunk.

With the $10,000, this group may then pay off Wells Fargo $4,000 and Capital One for $6,000. (Right away, this is the wrong combination of debts to pay, but we will ignore the mistake for this example.) Paying off Capital One and partially bringing down the balance of Chase Sapphire would in no doubt present a better outcome in terms of reducing interest costs while amassing the same, exact cash flow gains, but again we will ignore this little mistake and accept that Wells Fargo and Capital One are both now paid off.

Here is the new, adjusted Excel worksheet after the payments were applied by the other group:

List of Debts	Limit	APR	Bal Owed	Min.	Avail	Credit Utilization	Payment Rate Charged	Term In Years
Wells Fargo Platinum	5,000	20.00%	0	0	5,000	0.00%	0.00%	
Capital One credit card	7,230	24.00%	0	0	7,230	0.00%	0.00%	
Chase Sapphire Pref	11,364	21.00%	10,000	200	1,364	88.00%	2.00%	
NavyFederal Loan	21,000	2.50%	21,000	460	-	100.00%	2.19%	4
Regions HELOC	50,000	3.99%	40,000	133	10,000	80.00%	0.33%	1 of 10
Interfirst Mortgage	116,350	3.99%	116,000	806	350	99.70%	0.69%	30

	Old figures	Adjustment	New Figures
Income:	$2,500		$2,500
Expense:	$2,300	$200	$2,100
Debts:	$187,000		$187,000
Cash flow/Money leftover:	$200	$80 + $120	$400

Now Wells Fargo and Capital One are paid off completely.

The minimum payments for Wells Fargo and Capital One got rolled over to the cash flow. Cash flow/extra payment has now increased from $200 to $400.

The velocity banking group's next goal could now be to bring the Regions HELOC balance down so at some point they could execute another chunk or large payment. This, right here, is one of the major problems facing this group. The concept is not going to work in this instance and will not yield greater interest cost savings. Our cash flow is better served somewhere else. Simply put, cash flow should go to a different account or debt; however, we will continue to allow to some extent the movements of income and expenses from this alternative account.

Out of the remaining debts on the board, let us compare Chase credit card with Regions HELOC. To have an apples-to-apples comparison, we will employ Ambroise's partitioning the balance of Regions HELOC

$40,000:

$30,000 at 3.99% or $1,197 yearly interest

+ $10,000 at 3.99% or $399 yearly interest

$40,000 at 3.99% or $1,596 yearly interest

To keep math simple, we will compute over the course of one year.

Chase Sapphire—$10,000 at 21%, 10,000 x 21/100 or $2,100 in interest charges per year

Regions HELOC—$10,000 at 3.99, 10,000 x 3.99/100 or $399 in interest charges per year

As you can see, over the course of one year, we will get killed with interest charges on the Chase Sapphire credit card. We cannot in good conscience support making extra payment, sending cash flow to a lower interest rate line instead of the higher interest rate line. It is true that using the Regions HELOC as a debt weapon will provide a reduced, overall effective interest rate or a reduction in interest costs, but the difference in interest charges compared to Chase Sapphire preferred credit card is too large to overcome. We will illustrate all of this in a moment.

This is another major distinction between what we are doing with our method compared to what the other side is doing in terms of which debt gets to keep the cash flow or extra payment at the end.

Can we still use Regions HELOC as a debt weapon or an ADAWA account to some extent? Yes, absolutely!

In general, when choosing an ADAWA account between one that offers greater liquidity and another that offers greater results in reducing interest costs, we will at a minimum start with the latter as a FIRST IN LINE alternative account or FIRST IN LINE to receive income/payment. However, there are instances where we may utilize multiple, active alternative/ADAWA accounts for simultaneous movements of income and expenses.

List of Debts	Limit	APR	Bal Owed	Min.	Avail	Credit Utilization	Payment Rate Charged	Term In Years
Wells Fargo Platinum	5,000	20.00%	0	0	5,000	0.00%	0.00%	
Capital One credit card	7,230	24.00%	0	0	7,230	0.00%	0.00%	
Chase Sapphire Pref	11,364	21.00%	10,000	200	1,364	88.00%	2.00%	
NavyFederal Loan	21,000	2.50%	21,000	460	-	100.00%	2.19%	4
Regions HELOC	50,000	3.99%	40,000	133	10,000	80.00%	0.33%	1 of 10
Interfirst Mortgage	116,350	3.99%	116,000	806	350	99.70%	0.69%	30

	Old figures	Adjustment	New Figures
Income:	$2,500		$2,500
Expense:	$2,300	$200	$2,100
Debts:	$187,000		$187,000
Cash flow/Money leftover: $200		$80 + $120	$400

The main question now is, which account or debt truly deserves to keep the cash flow/ extra payment at the end?

Let us continue by mimicking the velocity banking concept or method to some extent:

List of Debts	Limit	APR	Bal Owed	Min.	Avail	Credit Utilization	Payment Rate Charged	Term In Years
Wells Fargo Platinum	5,000	20.00%	0	0	5,000	0.00%	0.00%	
Capital One credit card	7,230	24.00%	0	0	7,230	0.00%	0.00%	
Chase Sapphire Pref	11,364	21.00%	10,000	200	1,364	88.00%	2.00%	
NavyFederal Loan	21,000	2.50%	21,000	460	-	100.00%	2.19%	4
Regions HELOC	50,000	3.99%	40,000	133	10,000	80.00%	0.33%	1 of 10
Interfirst Mortgage	116,350	3.99%	116,000	806	350	99.70%	0.69%	30

	Old figures	Adjustment	New Figures
Income:	$2,500		$2,500
Expense:	$2,300	$200	$2,100
Debts:	$187,000		$187,000
Cash flow:	$200	$80 + $120	$400

Let us first run the scenario where the Regions HELOC *keeps* the $400 cash flow or extra payment completely. In other words, $2,500 income comes in and only $2,100 expense goes out to pay down/off debts. This is the typical route the other group usually takes, even though it may not be practical in real life since most Americans who are on a biweekly pay schedule do not receive their overall, total income all at once.

HELOC Current Balance:	40000
Interest Rate:	3.99%
Daily Rate:	4.3726
Income comes in (-):	2500
Result:	37500
Interest Rate:	3.99%
Daily Rate:	4.0993
Expense goes out (+):	2100
Result:	39600
Interest Rate:	3.99%
Daily Rate:	4.3289
Average Daily Total:	4.2669
Number of days in given month:	30
Monthly Interest charges:	**128.01**
Effective Rate:	3.89%

List of Debts	Limit	APR	Bal Owed	Min.	Avail	Credit Utilization	Payment Rate Charged	Term In Years
Wells Fargo Platinum	5,000	20.00%	0	0	5,000	0.00%	0.00%	
Capital One credit card	7,230	24.00%	0	0	7,230	0.00%	0.00%	
Chase Sapphire Pref	11,364	21.00%	10,000	200	1,364	88.00%	2.00%	
NavyFederal Loan	21,000	2.50%	21,000	460	-	100.00%	2.19%	4
Regions HELOC	50,000	3.99%	40,000	133	10,000	80.00%	0.33%	1 of 10
Interfirst Mortgage	116,350	3.99%	116,000	806	350	99.70%	0.69%	30

	Old figures	Adjustment	New Figures
Income:	$2,500		$2,500
Expense:	$2,300	$200	$2,100
Debts:	$187,000		$187,000
Cash flow:	$200	$80 + $120	$400

Let us now run another scenario where Regions HELOC *does not* keep the $400 cash flow. In other words, $2,500 income comes in and the same $2,500 in expense goes out to pay down debts, including the Regions HELOC regular monthly payment. This is unusual because all the income comes into the Regions HELOC, and all the expenses go out of the account; it's a wash. Regions HELOC effective interest rate for the given month still got reduced; however, another account, Chase Sapphire preferred credit card, keeps the $400 cash flow or extra payment.

HELOC Current Balance:	40000
Interest Rate:	3.99%
Daily Rate:	4.3726
Income comes in (-):	2500
Result:	37500
Interest Rate:	3.99%
Daily Rate:	4.0993
Expense goes out (+):	2500
Result:	40000
Interest Rate:	3.99%
Daily Rate:	4.3726
Average Daily Total:	4.2815
Number of days in given month:	30
Monthly Interest charges:	**128.45**
Effective Rate:	3.91%

List of Debts	Limit	APR	Bal Owed	Min.	Avail	Credit Utilization	Payment Rate Charged	Term In Years
Wells Fargo Platinum	5,000	20.00%	0	0	5,000	0.00%	0.00%	
Capital One credit card	7,230	24.00%	0	0	7,230	0.00%	0.00%	
Chase Sapphire Pref	11,364	21.00%	10,000	200	1,364	88.00%	2.00%	
NavyFederal Loan	21,000	2.50%	21,000	460	-	100.00%	2.19%	4
Regions HELOC	50,000	3.99%	40,000	133	10,000	80.00%	0.33%	1 of 10
Interfirst Mortgage	116,350	3.99%	116,000	806	350	99.70%	0.69%	30

	Old figures	Adjustment	New Figures
Income:	$2,500		$2,500
Expense:	$2,300	$200	$2,100
Debts:	$187,000		$187,000
Cash flow:	$200	$80 + $120	$400

In both scenarios, whether Regions HELOC keeps or does not keep the $400 cash flow/extra payment, the 3.99% APR rate for Regions HELOC got reduced essentially for the given month.

When HELOC keeps the $400 cash flow, total interest charges for the month are $128.01. When HELOC does not keep the $400 cash flow, total interest charges for the month are $128.45.

The difference in interest cost savings for using the $400 cash flow is ($128.45 - $128.01) or $ 0.44 plus the interest cost savings on the $400 payment itself, so ($400 x 3.99% /12) or $1.33. Thus, Regions HELOC behind the scenes would save a combined, total interest of ($1.33 + $0.44) or $1.77.

The question now is, can we do better than *$1.77* in interest cost savings for the month if we send the $400 cash flow to pay down a different account, a different debt. Well, let us find out: We know for each dollar borrowed, Chase in our example will charge us 21% a year. The reverse is true for each payment made; we will save 21% in interest for the year.

If we send the $400 cash flow as an extra payment to Chase Sapphire preferred credit card at 21%, we will save 400 X 21% /12 or *$7* in interest savings for the given month.

As you can see, cash flow sent to pay down Chase credit card will save $7 in interest costs. If Regions HELOC keeps the cash flow, we will save a depressing $1.77 in combined, total interest cost savings from two different places using velocity banking for the month.

The Verdict: Send *at least* $400 cash flow to the highest APR line, Chase Sapphire credit card, for the given month if you belong to the velocity banking group.

Ambroise method 1.0 follows a totally separate, unrelated process, which we will demonstrate shortly. Ambroise method 1.0 is abundant with numerous strategies and techniques that were previously unheard of in the year 2023.

Also in the near future, we plan to show you in greater detail how to utilize not just two but possibly three separate alternative accounts simultaneously for maximum interest savings. And we will show you how to correctly pay off mortgage faster, and dive deeply into the possible danger associated with cash back rewards while paying down debts as part of the topics that will be covered on our future, advanced version, Ambroise Method 2.0.

So far, we have covered which account may get to keep the cash flow or extra payment if we belong to the velocity banking group. Now let us cover the other potential problems with movements of income and expenses from that account.

Earlier, we mentioned that while an individual is waiting to receive the next biweekly paycheck or income, the bills have not stopped, they keep coming, or are due throughout the month. This may create problems in this alternative account when expenses going out surpass income coming in, even for a brief period. Too many expenses going out of the alternative account may increase the overall balance, which in turn will diminish the performance of that account. Remember that interest on a PLOC, HELOC, credit card, to name a few, are calculated mostly (average) daily. That can prove to get worse for people who are on commissions, salaries, or irregular-type paychecks. To alleviate this problem to some extent, one option is to change the respective due dates of those bills; however, this may not solve anything. It depends on the type of pay period you are in and the small financial emergencies that always seem to arise. Another option is to charge your credit card for bills that can go on a credit card, then pay at least the statement balance on the given credit card on or before the due date. Here a possible residual interest or trailing interest may create problems.

Now let us see what happens to this alternative account if expenses flagrantly got taken out (to pay bills) before any paychecks or overall total income arrives, whether that alternative account has an integrated sweep checking account feature like an all-in-one loan or some first lien HELOCs. (In this example, Regions HELOC will keep the cash flow/extra payment at the end.)

Regions HELOC Current Balance:	40000
Interest Rate:	3.99%
Daily Rate:	4.3726
If expense goes out first (+):	2100
Result:	42100
Interest Rate:	3.99%
Daily Rate:	4.6022
And Income comes in last (-):	2500
Result:	39600
Interest Rate:	3.99%
Daily Rate:	4.3289
Average Daily Total for all:	4.4346
Number of days in given month:	30
Monthly Interest charges:	133.04
Effective Rate:	**4.05%**

This is not good! Regions HELOC rate initially was 3.99%. Its new effective interest rate has now increased to 4.05% for the given month. As you can see, any debt repayment method that uses an alternative account can be a good concept; however, the timing of income coming into that alternative account and expenses going out of that account should be carefully examined. In addition, which account at a minimum gets to keep the cash flow or extra payment, just to name a few issues.

AMBROISE METHOD 1.0

You may first want to execute this strategy on paper for the very first month prior to starting any balance transfers online or placing phone calls to the creditors' customer service line.

There may be an impact to credit score.

Ambroise Method 1.0 calls for a series of steps that need to be taken at least monthly:

1. Segregate

Segregate the accounts by same account type (revolving credit with revolving credit—if PLOC/HELOC still have a draw period, well that is revolving, installment credit with installment credit).

2. Compare

Compare the accounts against one another by APR rates or interest charges over a certain period, usually in a year but could be shorter. America, here you will identify the biggest enemy, the troublemaker.

3. Transfer

Execute a balance transfer between the accounts if it makes (number, math) sense from biggest APR or interest charges into smallest APR or interest charges via:

a) Normal type of balance transfers

Denotes for our purpose balance transfers between same account type, e.g. revolving with revolving credit accounts or installment with installment credit accounts.

b) Artificial type of balance transfers

Denotes for our purpose unconventional, creative ways of transferring funds between either same or different account types while employing:

–Ambroise's charge-pay technique (normal)

for bills, expenses that either you or someone you know use cash for

–Ambroise's charge-pay technique (inducement)

for bills, expenses that either you or someone you know use cash for as well

–Plastiq, Melio, or similar entities for a fee

c) Mix & match type of balance transfers

Denotes for our purpose a transfer between a revolving and installment credit accounts.

Caution: Be extremely careful with federal or private student loan(s) due to the possibility of losing some benefits for paying the student loan(s) down or off via a refinance, consolidation, or balance transfer.

4. Repeat

After comparing then transferring between accounts, the new adjusted accounts become our new starting point. We will repeat the process of comparing, then transferring between accounts if it makes (number, math) sense while estimating our possible large payment, if any, toward debts or our total cash flow/extra payments second from a regular checking/savings account or ADAWA account.

Ambroise Method 1.0 in part is rearranging, reorganizing all our debts first for maximum interest savings before we either send in a large payment amount or cash flow/extra payment toward debts. In other words, we first rearrange and reorganize whenever possible all of our debts from our combined debt lists before any other type of payments toward debts can be applied.

Condition, Exception, Restriction to the Strategy

On very rare occasion, we may have the ability to send in a large payment toward debts from the very beginning of the debt repayment process, and if the large payment was sufficient to pay down/off most of these accounts initially, then we may do just the right number of additional balance transfers or no additional balance transfers at all. Any prior, existing enrollment for automatic bill payments from one account may have to be changed, or moved to a different account on the list.

Additionally, we may have an event priority where paying down/off one debt takes precedence over paying down/off a different debt outside the normal result of our plan or process.

Ambroise Method 1.0 (Continued)

Only after the four strategies above (segregate, compare, transfer, repeat) have been exhausted, no longer made (number, math) sense, or were not used at all due to condition, exception, or restriction to the strategies, can the next step occur, which is to ask the questions:

Can we send in a large payment?	or	Can we only use extra payment/cash flow?
If sending in a large payment is a *yes*, then which account to use (checking, savings)		If we can only send in an extra payment, then which account to use (checking, savings)
or		or
Which ADAWA account(s) to use?		Which ADAWA account(s) to use?
How much of a payment to send?		How much of a payment to send?
To pay down/off which debt(s)?		To pay down/off which debt(s)?
(Comparing the accounts against one another by APR rates or interest charges over a certain period of time, usually in a year but could be shorter.)		(Comparing the accounts against one another by APR rates or interest charges over a certain period of time, usually in a year but could be shorter.)

If you prefer to use your normal checking or savings account, this method is perfect for you.

If you like to use an alternative deposit or alternative withdrawal account, you may get a better result.

This method is also perfect for you!

Now, let us illustrate with this case study:

List of Debts	Limit	APR	Bal Owed	Min.	Avail	Credit Utilization	Current Term In Years
Capital One Credit Card	8000	26.99%	7274	257	726	90.93%	
USAA Credit Card	9000	22.15%	8010	225	990	89.00%	
Navy Fed Credit Card	25000	15.00%	5000	122	20000	20.00%	
Penfed HELOC	71000	9.25%	70000	497	1000	98.59%	10-20 (year 1 of 10)
Regions HELOC	99000	8.13%	93000	837	6000	93.94%	10-20 (year 1 of 10)

Income/Take-Home Pay:	$4,880
Expense:	$4,680
Debts:	$183,284
Cash flow/Money leftover:	$200

Note: All the above listed credit cards offer balance transfers, and the rate is the same as the purchase rate or the APR. Balance transfer fee is at 0%, and transfers are capped at 75% of the credit limit. However, some of the $4,680 in expenses are bills that cannot be paid with a credit card instantly. The real estate investor/client thinks that only $1,467 of bills can go on a credit card instantly without the use of any creative techniques (please see artificial type of balance transfers), and he will provide me with these figures as soon as he knows them for sure.

The other debt repayment methods will usually spend months or years keeping debt(s) at a higher interest rate (APR) or interest charges since their aim is to work on one debt at a time or a few small debts at a time. Here, to the extent that we can, we don't like to spend an extra day, month, or year babysitting a debt at a higher interest rate (APR) or interest charge. Our goal in part is to aggressively go after debts, reducing our overall interest charges, and in turn surpassing the results of any other debt repayment methods and possibly gaining the largest amount of cash flow or extra payments in the process. We have a wholistic approach on how we tackle debts from our combined, existing debt lists. Here is what we mean:

First, let us Segregate:

This process is already complete; all the accounts on the board are revolving credit type.

Next, let us Compare:

By APR in this example, Capital One has the biggest APR, and Regions HELOC has the smallest APR.

Next, let us Transfer:

From the absolute biggest APR to the absolute smallest APR (for maximum interest savings).

The real estate investor client is comfortable to go up to 98.50% of Regions HELOC limit (saturation point) $99,000 x 98.50%, minus current balance of $93,000, so $4,515 is available for balance transfer.

Now let us execute a balance transfer or payment of $4515 from Regions HELOC to Capital One.

After we have made the payment from Regions to Capital One credit card, Regions HELOC balance will increase by the amount of the charge of $4,515, and Capital One balance will decrease by the amount of the payment of $4,515.

Our Excel worksheet so far should look like this after the transfer:

List of Debts	Limit	APR	Bal Owed	Min.	Avail	Credit Utilization
Capital One Credit Card	8000	26.99%	2759	97	5241	34.49%
USAA Credit Card	9000	22.15%	8010	225	990	89.00%
Navy Fed Credit Card	25000	15.00%	5000	122	20000	20.00%
Penfed HELOC	71000	9.25%	70000	497	1000	98.59%
Regions HELOC	99000	8.13%	97515	878	1485	98.50%

Now both Regions and Penfed HELOCs are close to being maxed out (saturation point). Now we move on to the next highest and smallest APR debts for another transfer. Again, our method attempts to tackle every single debt from our combined, existing debt lists. We do not toy with the debts like the other methods are doing, working on one or two small debts at a time. We aggressively try to reorganize and rearrange all the highest APR rate or interest charged debts and work on multiple debts at a time on the same given day sometimes.

Next, let us Repeat:

Since Regions and Penfed HELOCs are now saturated, the next highest and smallest APR debts are Capital One and Navy Federal. However, Navy Fed is capped at 75% of credit limit for balance transfers.

Twenty-five thousand x 75% capped, minus current balance of $5,000, so $13,750 is available for balance transfers.

Therefore, we will transfer $2,759 from Capital One and zero out that account in the process. We will transfer $8,010 from the next highest card, USAA, and zero out that account in the process.

Navy Federal used up to $10,769 of the $13,750 available to zero out the above accounts, Capital One credit card and USAA credit card.

Putting it all together, our Excel worksheet should look like this:

List of Debts	Limit	APR	Bal Owed	Min.	Avail	Credit Utilization
Capital One Credit Card	8000	26.99%	0	0	8000	0.00%
USAA Credit Card	9000	22.15%	0	0	9000	0.00%
Navy Fed Credit Card	25000	15.00%	15769	385	9231	63.08%
Penfed HELOC	71000	9.25%	70000	497	1000	98.59%
Regions HELOC	99000	8.13%	97515	878	1485	98.50%

	Old figures	Adjustments	New Figures
Income/Take-Home Pay:	$4,880		$4,880
Expense:	$4,680	$178	$4,502
Debts:	$183,284		$183,284
Cash flow/Money leftover:	$200	$178	$ 378

It is worth repeating that other debt repayment methods will usually spend months or years keeping debt(s) at a higher interest rate (APR) or interest charges since their aim is to work on one debt at a time or a few small debts at a time. Here, to the extent that we can, we don't like to spend an extra day, month, or year babysitting a debt at a higher interest rate (APR) or interest charge. Our goal in part is to aggressively go after debts, reducing our overall interest charges, and in turn surpassing the results of any other debt repayment methods and possibly gaining the largest amount of cash flow or extra payments in the process.

To recap, this is where we started:

List of Debts	Limit	APR	Bal Owed	Min.	Avail	Credit Utilization	Current Term In Years
Capital One Credit Card	8000	26.99%	7274	257	726	90.93%	
USAA Credit Card	9000	22.15%	8010	225	990	89.00%	
Navy Fed Credit Card	25000	15.00%	5000	122	20000	20.00%	
Penfed HELOC	71000	9.25%	70000	497	1000	98.59%	10-20 (year 1 of 10)
Regions HELOC	99000	8.13%	93000	837	6000	93.94%	10-20 (year 1 of 10)

This is where we are so far after rearranging and reorganizing our combined, existing debt lists:

List of Debts	Limit	APR	Bal Owed	Min.	Avail	Credit Utilization
Capital One Credit Card	8000	26.99%	0	0	8000	0.00%
USAA Credit Card	9000	22.15%	0	0	9000	0.00%
Navy Fed Credit Card	25000	15.00%	15769	385	9231	63.08%
Penfed HELOC	71000	9.25%	70000	497	1000	98.59%
Regions HELOC	99000	8.13%	97515	878	1485	98.50%

The result above so far was simply from rearranging and reorganizing our combined debts from our existing debt lists. All of this can be done in a few minutes online, or worst-case, in a couple hours by placing a phone call to the creditor's customer service line.

We have not even begun to utilize our cash flow/extra payment to send toward debts, which is where the other three popular debt repayment methods usually start.

Their starting point, for the most part, is to throw cash flow/extra payment or large payment at one debt. Our starting point is to first rearrange and reorganize most, if not all, of our internal, global list of debts.

As you can see, based on the numbers alone, we are already ahead in terms of interest savings.

Ambroise Method 1.0

(Method of Peace & Reconciliation)

America, please pay attention to what just happened after rearranging and reorganizing the debts. Our highest APR rate debt remaining is now Navy Federal credit card (debt avalanche). Our smallest balance owed debt remaining is also Navy Federal credit card (debt snowball).

These two camps (debt snowball and debt avalanche) seldom get the same result. Our process of rearranging and reorganizing debts was able to get them into agreement. We have brought unity to these two camps. America, you know that we were able to devise a great method when we could for a moment get these two camps to agree with each other.

Let us get back to our example:

List of Debts	Limit	APR	Bal Owed	Min.	Avail	Credit Utilization
Capital One Credit Card	8000	26.99%	0	0	8000	0.00%
USAA Credit Card	9000	22.15%	0	0	9000	0.00%
Navy Fed Credit Card	25000	15.00%	15769	385	9231	63.08%
Penfed HELOC	71000	9.25%	70000	497	1000	98.59%
Regions HELOC	99000	8.13%	97515	878	1485	98.50%

	Old figures	Adjustments	New Figures
Income/Take-Home Pay:	$4,880		$4,880
Expense:	$4,680	$178	$4,502
Debts:	$183,284		$183,284
Cash flow/Money leftover:	$200	$178	$ 378

Now that the four strategies (Segregate, Compare, Transfer, Repeat) have been exhausted, the next step is to ask the questions:

Can we send in a large payment, or can we only use extra cash flow? The answer in our example is cash flow.

Then which account to use? For someone who prefers to use a regular checking or savings account, your answer will be either a checking or savings account.

However, for those who prefer to use some form of debt acceleration strategy, which ADAWA account(s) to use? You may have multiple accounts to choose from, so choose wisely. I will explain further below.

Keep these in mind!

	Navy Credit Card, in this example	Penfed HELOC, in this example
Type:	Revolving	Revolving in this case (draw period remaining)
Computation:	Average Daily	Average Daily
Liquidity:	Determined not to be as liquid	Greater liquidity (draw period remaining)
Term Left:	N/A	We are in year one of ten-year draw

In general, when choosing an ADAWA account between one that offers greater liquidity and another that offers greater results in reducing interest costs, we will at a minimum start with the latter as a FIRST IN LINE alternative account or FIRST IN LINE account to receive income/payment. However, there are instances where we may utilize multiple, active alternative/ADAWA accounts for simultaneous movements of income and expenses.

Now, if we are eyeballing the list of all the revolving credits that do not have a zero balance, Navy Fed credit card has considerably the highest APR rate or interest charges and therefore will offer us the greatest results in reducing interest costs. In other words, Navy Federal credit card will be **FIRST IN LINE** to receive income/payment up to the expenses amount that can go on a credit card. So tentatively $1,467 (this figure was provided to us by the client) plus new, total available cash flow amount of $378, plus its own minimum monthly payment amount of $385, for a grand total of $2,230.

Our FIRST IN LINE alternative account to receive income up to $2,230 is Navy Federal credit card.

PROOF: When income comes to the alternative deposit or alternative withdrawal account, it is equivalent to a payment, and we would want to send our payment to the highest APR rate or interest charged account to reduce that high interest, thus saving us interests substantially.

Let us determine which account will be our **NEXT IN LINE** alternative account?

Both Penfed and Regions HELOCs offer greater liquidity compared to Navy Federal credit card that instantly does not.

Between Penfed and Regions HELOCs, which one will become our NEXT IN LINE alternative account?

Well, the one with the highest APR rate or interest charges is Penfed, so we could reduce that interest rate even further when we have movements of income coming into that account and expenses going out of that account. In other words, Penfed HELOC will be NEXT IN LINE to receive income/payment in our given example. Penfed will receive its own minimum payment of $497, plus whatever amount that could not go on the Navy Federal credit card, about $2,153, so a grand total of $2,650.

This NEXT IN LINE Penfed HELOC behaves similarly to a regular checking account that will hold funds and expenses that cannot be paid with Navy Federal credit card instantly. The overall interest rate for Penfed HELOC will be reduced when we have movements of income and expenses in that account.

Caution: Don't forget that for best performance in reducing interest costs on most ADAWA accounts, income should always come first and be equal to, or greater than, expense amounts leaving that account.

It is important to mention that the other debt repayment methods like to toy with the debts or have a gentle approach in eliminating debts. Here at Ambroise Method 1.0, we aggressively go after the debts.

Again, in the near future we plan to show you in greater detail how to utilize not just two—but possibly three separate alternative accounts simultaneously for maximum interest savings. We will also show you how to correctly pay off mortgage faster, and we will dive deeply into the possible danger associated with cash back rewards while paying down debts as part of the topics that will be covered on our future, advanced version, Ambroise Method 2.0. Ambroise Method 1.0 emphatically beats the competition; imagine what Ambroise Method 2.0 will do!

Ambroise's Charge-Pay Technique (Normal)

You could artificially transfer balances from the highest APR rate account into the lowest APR account when the normal balance transfers cannot be obtained or when the balance transfer fee is too high.

Let me demonstrate by using the example below:

Charge-Pay Technique	Limit	APR	Bal Owed
Wells Fargo Credit Card	4820	15.00%	800
Chase Sapphire Credit Card	11364	21.00%	10000

Scenario: You have room in your Wells Fargo credit card to make a transfer; however, Wells Fargo is not offering any balance transfer promotions currently. What do you do?

For expenses that either you, your family member, your friend, or your co-worker usually pay for with cash, let us say the total for those expenses is $3,750, and those expenses can go on your credit card. Well, collect the cash from yourself or from your friends and family and temporarily deposit the cash into your checking or savings account, but instead of continuing to use cash for those expenses, charge your lowest APR card. In this case, it is Wells Fargo so Wells Fargo balance will increase by the amount of the charges of $3,750. Then pay your highest APR card with the cash that you have collected and set aside. In this example, pay Chase Sapphire. The balance of Chase Sapphire will decrease by the amount of the payment of $3,750.

Your new, adjusted Excel worksheet will look like this:

Charge-Pay Technique	Limit	APR	Bal Owed
Wells Fargo Credit Card	4820	15 00%	4550
Chase Sapphire Credit Card	11364	21 00%	6250

Here, you will take full advantage of the difference in APR rate:

(21%–15%) or 6% of interest savings

The result is essentially a balance transfer; however, you did not pay any balance transfer fee in this example where you have charged one account, then paid another account.

America, I am anticipating that the big banks and creditors are not going to be happy with me showing you this Ambroise's charge-pay technique. They will not be collecting any balance transfer fees, which represent an important source of revenue for the big banks and creditors.

Ambroise's Charge-Pay Technique (Inducement)

You are dedicated and want to save as much interest as possible while getting out of debt; however you are getting some pushback. Folks do not want to give you their cash. For this instance, an inducement of 1% may change their minds; they may now want you to have their cash.

Note: Under a normal balance transfer with the banks, they usually charge in 2023 between 1%– 5%.

This time you are charging yourself a smaller fee, 1%, to do the (artificial) balance transfer. The balance transfer will now cost you 1% of $3,750 or $37.50.

Before you proceed, will this be a good move? America, how long will it take for us to recoup the inducement/fee of $37.50 we plan to pay to receive the cash from our friends and/or family?

Charge-Pay Technique	Limit	AFR	Bal Owed
Wells Fargo Credit Card	4820	15.00%	800
Chase Sapphire Credit Card	11364	21.00%	10000

Existing cash flow: $200

Let us run the numbers. To have an apples-to-apples comparison, we will have to partition the (bigger) balance of $10,000 from Chase $6,250 at 21%.

Wells Fargo $3,750 at 15%. You are saving 6% in interest here—$3,750 at 21% .

Chase $3,750 at 21% or $3,750 x 21% / 12 $65.625 monthly interest charges

Wells Fargo $3,750 at 15% or $3,750 x 15% / 12 $46.875 monthly interest charges

Interest savings for doing the balance transfer $18.75 difference in monthly savings

So, now how long to recoup the 1% inducement/fee or $37.50?

$37.50/$18.75 in monthly savings is equal to two payments or two months.

It will take two payments or two months to recoup the fee of 1% of $37.50.

Normal balance transfers

Artificial-type of balance transfers

Mix & match-type of balance transfers vs. using extra payment/cash flow

America, can we achieve the same thing by using our cash flow/extra payment instead so we will not have to do any balance transfers that may cost us between 1%–5% fee?

Let us run the numbers.

We know for each dollar borrowed, Chase in our example will charge us 21% a year or 1.75% a month. The reverse is true for each payment made; we will save 21% in interest or 1.75% a month in interest.

Now our available cash flow before any transfer is only $200. If we make a payment to Chase using our cash flow of $200, we will save $200 x 21%/12 or $3.50 in interest savings for the month.

Using our cash flow, we will only be saving $3.50 for the month. However, using Ambroise's charge-pay technique (Inducement), this artificial type of balance transfer will save us $18.75 in interest.

A Brief Introduction of Plastiq, Melio, or Other Similar Entities

Here are the statistics:

Sixty-four percent of Americans are living paycheck to paycheck.

Sixty-eight percent of Americans may not be able to cover a $400 emergency.

As you can see, you may not have enough cash flow or money leftover to make a dent on those debts. Can I create a method to still give you some relief, America?

In some cases, you may have to use unconventional techniques to achieve greater relief than what your extra payment or cash flow can provide.

Let me preface this by saying that as of the writing of this book, I have not nor have I ever received in the past any compensations from Plastiq. I have used their product in the past and it has worked wonderfully for me. Plastiq in part will charge your credit card a fee, then send either a wire, an ACH payment, or a check to your approved creditors. You may have to do your due diligence since there may be some restrictions as to which type of credit card you can use and what type of vendors or individuals you can send payments to. Plastiq, Melio, and other similar entities can be additional ways to create some (artificial) type of balance transfers for a fee in the year 2023.

Mix & Match Type of Balance Transfers

For our purpose, mix & match balance transfer is a transfer between a revolving credit and installment credit accounts.

Caution: Be extremely careful with federal or private student loan(s) due to the possibility of losing some benefits for paying the student loan(s) down or off via a refinance, consolidation, or balance transfer.

Now, let us assume that you have done your due diligence and already had one major credit card that is allowing you to move your student loan debt into the credit card. The credit card company is offering a promotional rate of 0% APR for 15 months with a 3% balance transfer fee.

Let us illustrate:

Mix & Match	Amount	APR	Bal.	Avail.	Monthly Payment Charged	Payment Rate Charged	Notes
Student Loan	20,000	5%	**5,000**	N/A	212	4.24%	10-year fixed
Credit Card	11,000	18%	**3,000**	8,000	60	2.00%	0% APR for 15 mo.; 3% bal. transfer fee

We will then transfer the student loan balance of $5,000 into the credit card. This will zero out the student loan balance on paper (there may still be some residual or trailing interests).

The credit card balance will then get increased by the amount of the transfer of $5,000.

The adjusted Excel worksheet will look like this:

Mix & Match	Amount	APR	Bal.	Avail.	Monthly Payment Charged	Payment Rate Charged	Notes
Student Loan	20,000	5%	**0**	N/A	0	0.00%	10-year fixed
Credit Card	11,000	18%	**8,000**	3,000	160	2.00%	0% APR for 15 mo.; 3% bal. transfer fee

We will amass a net positive cash flow of ($212+60) - $160 or $112 in additional cash flow.

America, how long will it take for us to recoup the balance transfer fee?

The fee was 3%; that is $5,000 x 3%, or $150 fee.

Installment credit interest is computed differently than revolving credit interest. Here is the breakdown for the student loan interest with a current balance of $5,000:

# of Payment	Monthly Payment Charged	Student Loan Interest	Principal	Ending Bal.
				$5,000
1	$212	$21	$191	$4,809
2	$212	$20	$192	$4,617
3	$212	$19	$193	$4,424
4	$212	$18	$194	$4,230
5	$212	$18	$195	$4,035
6	$212	$17	$195	$3,840
7	$212	$16	$196	$3,644
8	$212	$15	$197	$3,447
9	$212	$14	$198	$3,249
10	$212	$14	$199	$3,051
11	$212	$13	$199	$2,851
12	$212	$12	$200	$2,651

Total combined interest on student loan balance of $5,000 after 8 months, shown above, is $144.

Interest charged on credit card balance after 8 months with 0% APR rate: $5,000 x 0% x 8/12 or $0

Difference in interest savings after 8 months from the balance transfer is: ($144 - $0) or $144.

So now how long to recoup the 3% fee or $150 ? X = $150

Eight months = $144

X = (150 x 8) / 144 or 8.33 months.

It will take a little over eight months to recoup the fee of 3%, or $150.

Here, we are not even taking into account the additional $112 in cash flow gains that was previously realized.

Note: Don't forget to quickly get rid of the original $5,000 balance prior to the 15-month promotion expiring; otherwise, you will go backward for swapping a low interest charged account for a high interest charged account.

In conclusion, throughout this book we have made a conscientious effort not to inflate the numbers from any original examples or case studies in order to make our results look more impressive. We have gone over various scenarios and provided you with a great visual picture of some of the deficiencies or pitfalls that may be associated with the other debt repayment methods and how we may be able to fix these issues. Our method, to some extent, creates solutions to these potential problems. We believe our method is by far the greatest debt repayment method in America.

Ambroise Method 1.0 can be used in some other countries as well.

It is worth repeating that other debt repayment methods will usually spend months or years keeping debt(s) at a higher interest rate (APR) or interest charges since their aim is to work on one debt at a time or a few small debts at a time. Here, to the extent that we can, we don't like to spend an extra day, month, or year babysitting a debt at a higher interest rate (APR) or interest charge. Our goal in part is to aggressively go after the debts, reducing our overall interest charges and in turn surpassing the results of any other debt repayment methods while possibly gaining the largest amount of cash flow or extra payments in the process.

Our method is inclusively helpful for rich individuals, high income earners, the 64% of Americans who are living paycheck to paycheck, and the 68% of us who may not be able to cover a $400 emergency.

Furthermore, you are now armed with revolutionary strategies and techniques that were previously unheard of in 2023 in your fight against debts!

Here are quick descriptions of some of my new concepts and terminologies used in this book:

ADAWA Account:

Alternative deposit, alternative withdrawal account–account that works similarly to a checking account.

Ambroise Method 1.0:

A revolutionized debt repayment method that may offer greater results than other debt repayment methods in terms of interest savings or reducing overall interest costs.

Ambroise Method 2.0:

A more advanced version compared to Ambroise Method 1.0.

Ambroise's Charge-Pay Technique (Inducement):

A detailed process where you will charge one account, then pay another account with available cash on hand using some form of inducement or fee.

Ambroise's Charge-Pay Technique (Normal):

A detailed process where you will charge one account, then pay another account with available cash on hand.

Ambroise's Partitioning a Balance:

To divide a balance into at least two separate parts, where one of the parts will equal the other account or credit card balance we are trying to compare it with.

Artificial type of transfers:

A creative way of transferring funds between accounts.

Event priority:

A concept in which one event takes precedence over the normal result of a plan or process.

Eyeballing method:

A way of quickly comparing the performance of at least two separate accounts.

FIRST IN LINE

alternative account—for our purpose, it is the account that offers greater results in reducing interest costs compared to another alternative account on a given list.

Mix & Match Type of Transfers:

Balance transfers between a revolving and installment credit accounts.

Monthly Payment Charged:

The amount charged on an account to cover a specific period.

NEXT IN LINE

alternative account—for our purpose, it is the account that offers greater liquidity compared to another alternative account on a given list.

Payment Rate Charged:

The relationship between the monthly payment and the current balance owed.

God, in your infinite mercy, you still find ways to use me for a great cause. I hope that I continue to prove my Sonship!